# CONCRETE

*Poetry*

## OLIVIA NGOZI OSUOHA

Mwanaka Media and Publishing Pvt Ltd,
Chitungwiza Zimbabwe
*
*Creativity, Wisdom and Beauty*

Publisher: *Mmap*
Mwanaka Media and Publishing Pvt Ltd
24 Svosve Road, Zengeza 1
Chitungwiza Zimbabwe
mwanaka@yahoo.com
mwanaka13@gmail.com
www.africanbookscollective.com/publishers/mwanaka-media-and-publishing
https://facebook.com/MwanakaMediaAndPublishing/

Distributed in and outside N. America by African Books Collective
orders@africanbookscollective.com
www.africanbookscollective.com

ISBN: 978-1-77934-082-5
EAN: 9781779340825

© Olivia Ngozi Osuoha 2024

All rights reserved.
No part of this book may be reproduced or transmitted in any form or by any means, mechanical or electronic, including photocopying and recording, or be stored in any information storage or retrieval system, without written permission from the publisher

DISCLAIMER
All views expressed in this publication are those of the author and do not necessarily reflect the views of *Mmap*.

**APPRECIATION**

I really and truly appreciate a Kenyan sage and friend, who has been helpful in some forms of editing, like arranging the Table of Contents, and other things, in the person of Andrew Nyongesa.

**Prologue**

This book CONCRETE is a collection of poems by the author, Ngozi Olivia Osuoha. She wrote these words under certain conditions at work, home, events, morning, afternoon, night, depending on when the inspirations came in. They are heartfelt realities and explosions of emotions. They are readable, understandable, and experiential. Some of the poem here are equally dedicated to certain individuals by which they were inspired.

**Table of Contents**

Acknowledgement
Fresh Oil to Boil
Dear Diocese Sapele
The Silent Graveyard
The Universe Is on reverse
The mystery of fate
Lent, The Truest Valentine
On your marks, Get ready, Go!
Genesis and Nemesis
The Land is Boiling
I am not Afraid of Bat
Rhapsody of Realities
On this Day of History
A Memorial of Catastrophe
Today is World Writer's Day
They are women too
Mama the Torchbearer
Soon and Very Soon
How do I Tell God
The Batista Bombs
By Rivers of Babylon
The Disco Man
Duty Calls
Close to Hell
These Tiny Wings of Mine
Serene
Look Yonder

Heavy Duty
The Drain
Bamboo
The Jetty
The Container and Content
The Everest
Dark and Lovely
Happy International Women's Day
Sitting on their Mandate
The Other Side of Life
Fame in the Wood
My Dear Olivia
Diamonds are Forever
The Testimony of a Green Soul
We Move
The Rajis
The Veracity of a Noun
Extraordinary
Ignited
Three Years in the Big Heart
The Landmark of Events
The Empirical Formula of Tin
Pentecost
Stone of Help
Take Your Flowers
Pencil in the Hand of Creator
Blind Bat
Row the Boat
From Grace to Grass

Fare thee Well
Come Rain
Dear Malawi
Dear Abraham Lincoln
The Platinum Queen
The Rain Forest
Dear Inspector and Festival People
Greener Pastures
Under the Moonlight
Keep Going
I am not a Zombie

## FRESH OIL TO BOIL

We are nothing but flesh
Hence we gather afresh
That we may receive new oil
To toil, and foil the foe.

As we receive afresh
May we no longer be flesh,
Let this oil be the coil
To soil, and boil our woe.

Fresh oil we pray
As this flesh, we lay.

Fresh oil and the ray
That we see the way,
And work all the day.

Oil to boil even at night
That we may have clear sight;
To turn hurdles into pebbles
And troubles into marbles.

Lord, boil us in fresh oil
And coil this flesh,
Foil the foe's toil
And oil us to boil afresh.

Give the priest thy feast
And give the clergy no allergy,

Show the lay the way
Lock the flock, and shield thy field.

## DEAR DIOCESE OF SAPELE

Dear Diocese of Sapele
Happy Crystal anniversary
It's my third year under your shelter
Hence, I write you this love letter;

I have heard of the storms you weathered
And of your forms that almost withered,
I have heard of the babies you fathered
And of the norms you manly shouldered,
May your cap always be feathered.

Dear Diocese of Sapele
Happy *crystal* anniversary,
It is a new wake, so let it quake
Shake the lake and take the cake.

Dear Diocese of Sapele
Happy *crystal* anniversary,
Remember there is a stake
So if you fake the brake
You will break the make.

Dark, the day? Tough, the night?
Shaky, the way? Rough, the flight?
Barking, the ray? Enough, the fight!

Peace to the east, peace to the west
Peace to the south, peace to the north
Happy *crystal* anniversary

I wish you more than a centenary.

All hail the ancient city of Sapele.

And happy anniversary to the *Crystal Star*

## THIS SILENT GRAVEYARD

Behold, the elephants have become ants
And the dogs have turned frogs,
Men now look like the hen
And women behave like children,
Everywhere is as quiet as the graveyard.

Graves have become waves
And we crave for the cave
Chicks are now ticks
Kicking quickly and falling sick
Picking briefly the bricks,
How come everyone is dead silent?

Spirits hunger like flesh
Limits linger yet afresh,
Seas roar, lions yawn
Oceans soar, loins turn pawn
Still dead silence reverberates!

Ghosts now host humans
Posts dry and die most
Yet this angry peace hovers a deadly silence.

The air cheer up the hair
The chair air all in pair
This fairy tale is not fair to tell.

Tailors stain the sailors' suit
Wailers wake the widow's pursuit

Inhalers and exhalers joke on the choke
I say this graveyard will degenerate to smoke.

Boots stampede roots
Loots impede fruits
I bet this graveyard shall vomit!

Cohorts and robots assault
Pots and ports resort
Pans and cans import
Streams and dreams in realms of cream
Beams beam and dim
All sorts of assorted insult
Believe me this graveyard must vomit.

I marvel, as I watch the gravel unravel
Because this navel is not a ritual
When the archival shall become mutual.

Eagles sour from tour
Rifts crack their contour
Gifts back off by hour
Beatles drop more than four,
This peace is deadly.

Crying peace, mourning silence
Hunger alarms the crowd
Scarcity lauds the lords
This peace is a ticking bomb,
A graveyard of harmful ghosts
Terrifying lives and properties.

## THE UNIVERSE IS ON REVERSE

The universe is on reverse
To clean the menace of the furnace,
So lift up your face, let it surface.

The time is prime
Let go of the coloured indigo
Undergo through Trinidad and Tobago
Provided your cargo is not tobacco.

My love for you is from above
Move round, it is boundless
Prove, I have. Glove, I give limitless
No stove can roast my dove.

The universe is on reverse,
We are rooting to soothe you smoothly
With a verse not perverse
With a case of strong base,
And a vase of praiseworthy lace.

# THE MYSTERY OF FATE

In a part of the world where leadership is crazy
The round leather game kept the world busy,
In a continent where governance is cruel
Passion lighted the night without fuel.

From the desert of Africa, appeared the elephants, the antelopes, the lions, the camels, the leopards, the zebras, the scorpions, the stallions, the panthers, the dogs, the warriors, and the squirrels...
   Thank God, the Ivorians didn't have ovarian cancer.

From the Nile of Africa came the Pharaohs, the sharks, the crocodiles, the mambas and the pirates....
   Thank God, the Coast didn't collapse.

From the sky of Africa, came the eagles, the stars, the thunders, the cranes, and the hawks...
   Thank God it didn't rain.

For weeks, we all did seek
As the meek lowered the cheek
And watch the weak rise to peak.

The prices and sacrifices
The fun, pun, and run
The heads of our dead,
All, a huge surprise for the prize.

Football glued our eyeball
Its socket shocked the pocket,

From the reproach of the coach
To the crew and its screw,
From the prayers of the players
To the pans of the fans,
From the vices of the vice
To the residents and their presidents,
Yet passion echoed like the wall of Jericho.

The green toil on the orange soil
The kindred-spirit and the paternal calabash
The ancestral pot and the traditional lineage
The spiritual genealogy and the physical domain
All, an indigenous right of the black nativity.

The forest tamed the wild
The coast famed the tide
The child framed the pride
And the host gave a banquet-toast.

## LENT, THE TRUEST VALENTINE.

Pure, humble, royal a love
Sure, gentle, loyal a dove
Hard, battle, total a move
Card, mantle, rural to prove
Love, so costlier than gold
Bold, so deadlier than cold.

Present, bigger than Valentine
Valentine, sweeter than wine
Vine, larger than line;
Length, lengthier than lane
Lent, lenten at length.

Sober, melting like rubber
Supper, fulfilling like manna
Manner, soothing like dinner
Love, real as love
God, kind as God.

Real, not a robber
Seal, pot of copper
Deal, plot of pauper
Heal, slot of leper.

Season, of reason unique
Reason, of season transparent
Lent, a rent against each plague
That makes so opaque the treason of hell.

From shrove to the stove
Swollen, broken and frozen
Yet solemn in such a volume
And holy a proven token,
That no alien could have stolen.

Happy Valentine; a saint he is
Never paint him dark for bliss
Hence faint not, and bait none the trait.

Remember no cash can buy this ash
For it will either wear or tear
And no flash can ever make it wash.

Flesh and blood, bread and wine
The sacrament of divine government,
Instituted, restituted, constituted and atoned;

Pitch then your tent in the lenten season,
For the Eastertide is the truest valentine.

## ON YOUR MARKS! GET READY!! GO!!!

Step out and see your footsteps
Mark the world and let your footmarks print the footprints of men.

Note, and have each footnote.

Restore the store to the core, even if the whore swore for more sore.

Down the valley are the downtrodden, so break the glass and give them a class of breakthrough.

This town will be downtown if there are no stairs to go downstairs.

Ponder beyond and see yonder, for your hand is handsome to give and forgive.

Worry less about worrisome matters
Fear not about fearsome issues,
And don't be scared of the scar.

The table must not be comfortable
So if you delay, the pair could despair.

Look, the cook may not be a crook
And the rug may not be rugged or crooked
But the cap can form a capsule for the ring to be lost in the spring.

The sun can shine, yet there will be no sunshine because the day has ceased its ray.

The moon can also light, still there will be no moonlight because the night has blinded its sight.

So fold yourself against any blindfold, and hold your feet to meet the world. Behold the gold.

The dark summons the darkness, hence their might can fight the right and height.

Please swing to the other wing for the kingdom of the king is free, with freedom to star true stardom and bar boredom.

Dust yourself from the sawdust. The gold dust is a trust.

The cucumber is not cumbersome but its weariness is wearisome.

The league of colleagues can farm potatoes, but a foe can crush their toes.

Therefore a lonesome soul can tire but a tiresome sole can be gruesome.

Do not forsake brotherhood online or offline for the sake of linear equation or lunar pressure because livelihood can't thrive on solitude no matter the magnitude.

Hope for the rain and the rainbow,
Keep handy the rainboot and raincoat,

Then get ready to brainstorm any cankerworm.

Also wash your brain, so that you don't be brainwashed
Fish out the crayfish from the wish, let it be awesome, and full of awe.

Let the tray portray the room
Sweep the bedroom with a broom and let the couple bond in bundle.

Jet out to get a set
Let your pet wet your mind so that your mindset will not lag behind irrespective of what you find.

Life is a race, grace it with your face
Embrace it, and score some brace at your pace.

Always know that the world is the field, passion is the track, and running is the event.

So whether you are a track event athlete or field event competitor, just get on your marks, get ready, go!

# GENESIS AND NEMESIS

God's own state is on its own,
The land of beauty is very ugly.
 Home for all has no light for the nation.
And the land of promise rejected Moses and Aaron.

The pearl of tourism can neither tour nor pour wine.
The home of peace is in pieces, shattered and splintered.
The food basket of the nation is raining caskets.
And the glory of all lands is a gory sight to behold.

The people's paradise is being tossed like a dice.
And the big heart suffers constant heartache and heart attack.

The heartbeat of the nation is in coma.
The coal city is neither warm nor lively.
Salt of the nation is a disobedient Lot.
The land of honour and integrity is a horror in absurdity.

The jewel of the savannah has been stolen.
And the eastern heartland is hopeless.

The new world is a hell.

See, the center of commerce cannot commence business.
And the center of learning cannot discern growth or development.
The home of hospitality is in hostility and porosity.
Look, the confluence town cannot influence unity.
The land of equity does not come with clean hands.

And the state of harmony is in discord; disconnecting and dismembering.

There is nothing excellent at the center of excellence.
The home of solid minerals is solidly against precious stones.
And the power state cannot drive even a turbine.

The sunshine state is in darkness,
The gateway state has no gate hence gatekeepers are asleep.
The land of virtue has no living spring
And the pace-setter is lagging behind.

The home of peace and tourism is at war with self.
The treasure base of the nation is empty and baseless.

The seat of the caliphate is searching for the pyramid.
And the nature's gift to the nation is stunted.

Pride of the Sahel is shy in the well and ashamed in the cell.
Farming is our pride, no longer goes to farm due to banditry.

And the center of unity is deeply faulty and in raw enmity.

Hence a thirty-six year old is still seen as a capital child, and a family of thirty-six battles with capital corruption.

The land is green, they say. But the future certainly is uncertain.

## THE LAND IS BOILING

The land is boiling
The birds are so weak to sing
I can hear them, in their nest humming
Their feathers are wet and weary
They can neither fly nor cry,
The land is boiling.

The trees are still, and in peril
Like they are keeping a vigil
They are no more airy but weary,
I can hear them murmur.
The leaves are neither green nor bloomy
They tell a tale of horror
I can hear them, warn
The land is boiling.

The stars are dark
They can neither twinkle nor sparkle
I can hear them mourn.
The sun is silent
He can neither shine nor shout
I can hear him sob.
The moon is moody
She can neither laugh nor smile
I can hear her moan,
The land is boiling.

The skies are lamenting
The rains are weeping

The clouds are crying,
The heavens are dim
They no longer glow or blow
I can hear them, loud
The land is boiling.

The beasts are roaring and men are panting
Famine is chasing, and hunger is cheering
Lack is ruling, and want is leading
Need is governing, and pain is presiding
The land is boiling.

Noble men are hungry
Royal women are dirty
Innocent children are starving;
The land is boiling.

The land is boiling and men are bleeding
Women are screaming the land is boiling,
Children are dying; the land is bleeding!

The hood has no food
The room is in gloom
The doom appears to be soon
Except we bloom and blossom.

# I AM NOT AFRAID OF BAT

Black bird that loves the night
Big eyes that do not see
Light wings that cannot fly
Blind bat, blind Bartimaeus.

So vividly, I could remember that night
The second of August, during my Youth Service
That was our first and long encounter
Yes, around past two in the morning
Thank God, I killed you.

Bat, I am not afraid of you!

I am not afraid of bat
I am not a cat although
But I have a golden hat
And I lay on stainless mat.

Like a thief, you always come
At night, through the window
Yes, at wee, ungodly hours
To kill, steal and destroy
But God is always God.

In my room, I have a broom
For a chase, in case you come.

In my roughly three years here
I have killed and killed bats

So I am not afraid of bat.

Even on our fence above,
One big one got electrocuted
And more than four, I have killed
The last one was so fierce,
The chase, the fight, the fear, the shutdown;
Days later my body still ached.

I have not come to kill or harm
So I am not afraid of you,
For His eye is on the sparrow
And I know He watches me.

This government shall favour me,
So chase me not around like rat.

Witches and their crafts, I know not
Pitches and drafts, I only do plot
Frequencies and agencies, I cherish a lot
Queens and teens, I clean their rot,
So hear me well, let the poor breathe!

This government shall favour me
The change did not kill me
The next level never stopped me,
The renewed hope can't be that strong,
This government shall establish me.

Baby steps, teething pain
Crawling trouble, walking falls

Puberty pain, adulthood price
This government shall upgrade me.

The God of abandoned property
And the God of twenty pounds
The God of our forefathers;
He is still a miracle worker!

This government shall favour me and my family
We are not afraid of bat,
So live and let live.

A people survived annihilation.

# RHAPSODY OF REALITIES

Morning by morning, new movies we see; the consequences of tribe over competence.

The dews and fog of ignorance have taken us to cloud nine,
It is a new dawn, and blind eyes are opening
Now we know the rich also cry.

Weather for two, no one but you
The gods must be crazy. All, the audacity of a renewed hope.

We are no longer at ease because of the arrows of god
The center could no longer hold and things have fallen apart.
Before our own eyes, under our nose, the masquerade is telling us tales by moonlight.

Well, the professing interventionist is cooking with a benevolent pot, so he forgot that beheading Macbeth on the twelfth night will not stop Oliver Twist from asking for more.

In other words, whether Eze goes to school or not, everyone believes Obi is a boy.

So if a tribal pilot snatches a ballot box, chances are that passengers will get chicken pox, monkey pox, or bigots and maggots. Does it matter whose ox is gored?

Moreso, that Edet lives in Calabar does not guarantee a romance with Chike and the River.

"A baby can not be Mai, some people said. Idris can not lead us into battle. We must kill him"
Hence Peter, the labourer treads with caution because he is a trained thread trader.

Now, the forgone alternative and the opportunity cost, all a rhapsody of realities.

I tell you again, the atmosphere for miracles is not in the stratosphere.

Therefore, it is the gravity of a working faith that can pull down the oracle from the pinnacle to erase the obstacle.

Hitherto, the tribe and her bribe, the bride and her pride, the ride by her side, and the tide in the wide, all; a very cruel hand of fate.

So the rhyme in the rhythm of a crime especially at prime is that with time, it will produce a very soured lime without a dime.

Unfortunately, it is the rhapsody of realities.

Cruise or bruise, we are in for a long walk. Heaven only knows.

## ON THIS DAY IN HISTORY

On this day in history, the tortoise wore a turquoise shell to ring the hell bell...men, women, youths and people gathered to renew hope in their land.

But on this day in history, a selected manhood erected his manhood to rape and violet a people.

On this day in history, manhood mandated his manholes to slaughter and desecrate the neighborhood in broad daylight.

On this day in history, a certain manhood publicly castrated men of timbre and calibre.
Booths turned pools of blood, and ballots flooded.

On this day in history, escorts protected cohorts and mascots led robots.

Troops trooped out to dance naked like a cultural troupe, on this day in history.

On this day in history, volunteers became deers as they took to their heels.

On this day in history, Esau became a political thug, Judas collected thirty pieces of silver, and Haggai delivered Ishmael.

On this day in history, manhood released pitbulls, agents were oxidized and reagents ostracized.

On this day in history, manhood castrated all the stallions and made a mockery of them.

On this day in history, the choice became lice. And the labour was a stillbirth.

Manhood released the thief to Pontius Pilate, and barbarians devoured the historians as monsters mobbed the fosters.

On this day in history, manhood erected his manhood to mesmerize nationhood.

On this day in history, Delilah shaved, Judas kissed, Herod beheaded, Baal spoke and manhood maneuvered.

On this day in history, curtains dropped, blinds tore, gallows swallowed, marrows turned hollow as sorrows follow the fallow furrow.

Manhood fed men and women with his semen.

Fate, at the rate of probate with late mate in a state of hate at the gate.

On this day in history, a memorial of immeasurable and unthinkable cloud rained on the crowd.

The market square was deserted. Masquerades bought and sold at the detriment of a continent, yes on this day in history.

On this day in history, tribes were barred. Borders were sandy. Hoarders were handy. And heaven saw hell.

The tomb became a womb, it did not matter if you flew in from Rome. Many could not go home. Manhood!

On this day in history, brotherhood stood in the woods to challenge the status quo.

Manhood and his yacht, manhood and his bullion, manhood and the manhood's, all a blind virgin symbolizing injustice.

Of a truth, the rhapsody of realities are yet to come. And subsidy is not the remedy.

I tell you manhood is a tragedy because Food Crisis is beyond childhood and adulthood.

On this day in history, manhood, your eraser became a bulldozer. Swinging moods, just for your own selfish good.

A saint, stole
A thief, painted
An addict gave verdict.

Till this day in history, they have not gone back to fry akara, roast corn, make hair in the salon, visit the hospitals, grant amnesty to the jailed, dipped their legs in the lagoon, eat with pupils, or do those funny things that actually tell who they are.

On this day in history, manhood took the hood in hostage.

## A MEMORIAL OF CATASTROPHE

Rank by rank, they headed to the bank
But their heart sank at the prank
Because to be frank, the tank is empty.

The chief priest feasts on the least
On the new leaf, the thief inflicts grief, not a brief one.

A palmist and his palmistry, permutating a chunk of probability.

Sorcerers in sorceries and merchants
in machinations.

The taunt is on and the hunt is haunting.
The hut is hot, and the hurt is not halting any time soon.

Unfortunately, the brunt of the stunt they flaunt is gaining momentum, I hope it does not burst their scrotum, because the drum of rum cannot gum the vacuum, it must hum.

They lob the ball and lobby the baller.

Then score an own goal to steal the coal and leave a sore for the record.

There is no job for Bob yet the mob has come to rob.

A rapid deed to get rid of the troubled mid and place a lid on the grid.

So whoever sees these bees and their fees watches either in glee or flees.

Loans moan as debtors groan. Interests crest on chests and breasts, making them restless.

Guests become pests, scattering nests.
And the quests test the west.

A stormy blast revealing the cast and the caste. Crushing and flushing.

Turn by turn, it burns
An apocalypse without apostrophe,
A holocaust without horoscope.

But the psalmist in his chaplaincy, chanting. Praying psalms and saying prayers against such a memorial of catastrophe.

Rank by rank, they still did head to the bank
But their heart sank at such a prank
Because to be frank, the tank was empty.

Uneasiness in businesses, agonies in companies, investors in captors, creditors in tormentors, industries in queries.

Costs rise like dust, thrust lost and trust in rust. Hence lust, is a must.

A very frank prank. It is my turn, and that's enough a catalogue of catastrophic memory!


## TODAY IS WORLD WRITERS' DAY

Today is World Day of Writers, please kindly permit me to celebrate a certain Nigerian writer.

She is a poet, writer, hymnist and thinker.

She has published twenty six poetry books, including a hymnbook.

All these books were published outside Nigeria, and some of them are archived in the United States Library Of Congress.

A particular book of hers called *HERDSMENIZATION* published in Yorkshire is in the following Legal Deposit Libraries:

Bodleian Libraries of the University of Oxford
Cambridge University Library
The National Library of Scotland
The Library of Trinity College Dublin, the University of Dublin
The National Library of Wales.

She has published over three hundred and fifty pieces, articles and essays in more than fifty countries.

Her works have featured and appeared in more than one hundred and forty international anthologies.

Some of her poems have been translated into Arabic, Khloe, Vietnamese, Greek, Hindi, Italian, Russian, Romanian, Chinese, Serbian, Spanish, Scots, Polish, Assamese, Macedonian, Farsi, among other languages.

She has numerous Words On The Marble.

Lastly and specially, she equally wants to celebrate her parents: her first teachers, her first writers, and her priceless role models.

That African Girl calls herself The Village Girl. She is simply an introvert, who passionately enjoys her talent.

Please permit me to celebrate her on this year's occasion of the International World Day of Writers.

By the way, she is neither rich nor famous but she is your friend,

## THEY ARE WOMEN TOO

Today, we celebrate our relatives in the jungles, living like animals, juggling through life, unaware of science and technology, free from social media dramas.
May they receive light, they are women too.

Today, we remember our sisters bound by culture, tradition and religion. Hidden by veils, in veils, with veils and under veils. Those we neither know nor recognize.
May they receive light, they are women too.

Today, we remember our misguided sisters in brothels and hotels. Languishing in drugs, alcoholism and sex.
May they receive light, they are women too.

Today, we remember our lost sisters in cartels. The addicts, traffickers, syndicates and the likes.
May they receive light, they are women too.

Today, we remember our beloved friends behind bars. Those guilty, not guilty, tried, awaiting trail, convicted, and on death row.
May they receive light, they are women too.

Today, we remember our junkie-sisters, those in the psychiatric hospitals, sick-homes and different hidden corners of junkie-dom.
May they receive light, they are women too.

Today, we remember our sisters in captivity, far away from nativity, helpless, hopeless, ruined and mesmerized.
May they receive light, they are women too.

Today, we remember our friends on the street, naked, mad, dirty, stinking, useless and eating from the garbage.
May they receive light, they are women too.

Today, we remember our sisters who fell victims of the society. Sisters whose lives were cut short abruptly.
May their souls receive light, they were women too.

Today, we remember our mothers who died while giving birth.
May their creative and procreative souls receive perpetual light, they were women too.

Today, we remember all women who could not attain their dreams and their destined heights.
May light shine on them, they are women too.

Today, we remember all the teenagers, ladies and women who have sold themselves to madness, stupidity, nudity for and the love of money both offline and online.
May they receive light, they are women too.

Today, we celebrate all the female folks around the world, may light celestial quicken our mortal bodies, amen.

Happy International Women's Day

## MAMA THE TORCHBEARER

Nearer and dearer, hearer and rearer
Paver and saver, giver and achiever:
Bright in her sight, flight in her fight,
Light in her might, right in her plight
Tight in her wright, kite in her height
Mama; the great torchbearer.

You task yourself to tear the mask
And melt your wax to pay our tax,
You dribble the bubble and handle the bundle
Then cuddle the little and settle the humble,
Mama; the angelic torchbearer.

You saddle the wobble and rekindle the cattle
Then battle the dwindle and couple the noble,
You marble the candle on portable table
Then crumble the gamble to trouble the feeble,
Mama; the awesome torchbearer.

When we stumble and fumble, as gullible and fallible
And double our grumble, then you appear sensible, tolerable and responsible

Showing how flexible and incredible a torchbearer can be.

Mama; candle in the wind
Struggling the fierce horses.
Mama; mantle in the field
Fighting with and the unknown forces
Yet battle raging without chances
Still, mama racing beyond choices.

The ploughing ox, the treasury box
Terrible labour, triple harbour
Mama; an honourable torchbearer.

The heat of the feat and the seat of the beat
Candle amidst stain, brain behind each angle
Fire in the rain, and wire amidst pain
Mama; the beautiful torchbearer.

Burning, melting, hurting, yet lighting the world
Thirsting, hungering, crying, yet feeding the home
Lacking, wanting, needing, still giving solace
Praying, hoping, waiting, still providing succour
Mama; the unique torchbearer.

Mama, light and the lighter
Lamp and the lampshade,
Mama, candle and the candlestick
Nipple, kettle and the tea
Mama, torch and the torchbearer.

Charged and recharged by God

Light and lighted from above
A celestial and divine dove
So natural a vine on the move.

Please dear world, today put your lighters up
Let the champagne pop up for Mama
Fill her cup to the top
And let her crop never drop.

Please dear earth, blow Mama a kiss
Let her enjoy some bliss,
May she firmly stand
And sojourn deeply in the land.

Please heaven, give Mama a hug
Bless her for her godly role.

Thank you Dear Mama
Happy Mothering Sunday,
We appreciate.

## SOON AND VERY SOON

Soon, and very soon, the hungry hunter will face the angry tiger for political survival.

Soon, and very soon, the annoying antelope will have no antenna to connect to the brown envelope for his political currency.

Soon, and very soon, the chameleon will deceive the echelon of lions with colour. Yes, the rainbow of political colours.

Soon, and very soon, the cat and the rat that brought in the bat to mess up our mat will no more be fat. Yes, because they will lose the political chart and no one will chat them up any more.

Soon, and very soon, the umpire and the judge shall meet judgement, either before or after retirement. Then the political vampires will expire.

Yes, they flog the dog and the frog, and hug the bug because they will sleep on the rug.
But soon, and very soon, the digging shall be dug. And the drug will be logged out.

They blow and cry foul when the fowl is not against the owl. They are political pawns.

See starvation steering up to scatter the sorcerer. Salty political sauce.

See the audacity of scarcity, advancing with adversity to make them sterile upon how fertile they think they are. Political impotence.

They believe they can wake up any moment, and take the rake to make or break the snake. No, the serpent is ardent, in advent adventure coming for a political conscription.

They assume the tortoise cannot make any noise, because their cartridge is facing the partridge hence they lure him with porridge. Political motives.

See the zebra crossing, yet a certain Sandra of Libra zodiac with gross cobra is feeding the kangaroo in the zoo wearing no bra. Political seductress.

That lizard is a hazard, a bastard without no gizzard. Political pork. Dirty and unclean.

So the fool thinks he is cool in his pool, even while drenching his wool and stooling on his tool. Political daft.

Hence they send the mosquito to Pluto, and make a ridge inside the fridge to create a political comatose and steal the glucose.

Soon, and very soon, hunger shall not render the hundreds of million mute.
Rather prepare to listen and dance to the flute. It won't be cute so wear your parachute.

Very soon, sooner than later, starvation shall send the masses to Aso rock, to rock and roll. Yes, they will flock with the cock. Therefore, never mock what you can't block.

The masses can no longer bear the pain. I see them marching to the government house to be housed by the government. A torment or garment is awaiting.

I don't know how soon is the soon, but I know soon and very soon, the masses shall break the glass ceiling.

This feeling is not right. Somebody, show me some love.

## HOW DO I TELL GOD

How do I tell God that Baal has mounted the pulpit?
How?

How do I tell God that Saul has anointed Goliath?
How do I?

How do I tell God that the shepherds have unleashed swarms of locust on the field?
How do I tell?

How do I tell God that Mark, a supposed saint, has sold the ark of covenant?
How do I tell him?

How do I tell God that Ahab is in charge of the temple?
How do I tell God?

How do I tell God that Rehab is a rehabilitation center?
How?

How do I tell God that obededon has started the Armageddon?
How do I?

How do I tell God that Lucifer is still leading praise and worship?
How do I tell?

How do I tell God that Joseph is accusing Mary of infidelity?
How do I tell him?

How do I tell God that prayer warriors are now charging and billing for and before prayers?
How do I tell God?

How do I tell God that the watchmen are drinking and dancing, partying and making merry?
How?

How do I tell God that the tares have outgrown the seeds?
How do I?

How do I tell God that the two by two disciples have become tourists and sightseers?
How do I tell?

How do I tell God that the dove has abandoned the mission to check the water level?
How do I tell him?

How do I tell God that the remnant has broken the covenant?
How do I tell God?

How do I tell God that they are still building that tower?
How?

How do I tell God that Moses has quenched the burning bush?
How do I?

How do I tell God that Adam is still strolling while Eve and the serpent still wine and dine, hence the home is turbulent?
How do I tell?

How do I tell God that me too, I have fallen?
How do I tell him?

How do I tell God that the world has been conquered?

How?
How do I?
How do I tell?
How do I tell him?
How do I tell God?

What do I tell God?
Where do I start?

## THE BATISTA BOMBS

It is a real WrestleMania, so we have to pay per view.

Unfortunately, some took the fast lane and ended up paying for hell in a cell.

Yeah, it is a battleground so we do not expect a royal rumble.

We remember that the elimination chamber is also a survivor-series, so we hang in.

We are aware that if we go for the money in the bank there will be nothing like "I quit" or "submission" because there will definitely be extreme rules.

We know that a SummerSlam is a SmackDown as well. So we embrace the slam, the smack, the down, and the syndrome.

The payback from tables, ladders and chairs is that the last man standing would be crowned at the night of champions. Simple!

By the way, the adverts were dementia and WrestleMania. The crowd cheered in expectations. The labour of a renewed hope. We move!

So from a cut angle, I would be the undertaker with sudden awakening and sharp comebacks, even until victory.

In other words, you can't see me for any type of spear whether from Goldberg or from the opportunist. The wall of Jericho has fallen!

Let us always bear in mind that the ring and the wrestle is for everybody, be you an entertainer or a performer. It is a stage.

Therefore, until then, let the bat keep flying like Ray Mysterio, while fans and spectators partake in and from the Batista bombs.

## BY THE RIVERS OF BABYLON

By the rivers of Babylon, bat the baptist is baptizing the land,
No creed, no deed
Just a baptism of greed and weed.

By the rivers of Babylon, bat the baptist is erecting a tribal stand
No food, no good
Just a baptism of wood burning the hood and swinging every mood.

By the rivers of Babylon, bat the baptist is subsidizing the fares
No care, no ware
Just a baptism of bees and fees.

By the rivers of Babylon, bat the baptist is confirming his words
Wider net, larger catch, bigger fish
Just a baptism of taxation and inflation.

By the rivers of Babylon, bat the baptist is occupying till he cums
No plus, no surplus
Just a baptism of minus and minimum.

By the rivers of Babylon, bat the baptist is borrowing and sorrowing
Just a baptism of loan and credit, debt and debit.

By the rivers of Babylon, bat the baptist has a tag, a bag and a rag, to gag and drag any nag,
Just a baptism of sag, wag and lag.

By the rivers of Babylon, there we sat, off bat the baptist
And there, we swept and slept
When the wicked left with our cleft
And there we wept for the theft:
How can we labour in a barren land?

Then like the zionite I pray; so let the words of my mouth
And the meditations of my heart
Be acceptable in thine sight, oh Lord!

## THE DISCO MAN

To the disco man that wears a flowered suit
I have not come to file another suit,
However, I have my own taste
And now I do cringe at your paste.

You display creed and caste
You will not hesitate to waste,
Hence I withdraw in a haste.

Dance your disco in court and club
Rob the fault on that bub,
Tear on, tear on like a cub.

I would rather travel to Limpopo
And feed on potato,
While you dance your disco in court.

To that man that wears a colourful suit
The rainbow used to be beautiful,
I will waste no time on that paste.

The caste will always be in a haste
In a hurry to fly and flaunt colour,
But always empty of empathy.

Dance your disco, but inhumane
They are all in an insane lane.

A profane disco, disco in court.

But life can deny Dennis of his penis
And let the tennis get lost in the crowd.

## DUTY CALLS

Here is the man
To boldly chair the table
And rotate the fan
For it not to wobble,
That is the fact
Please give him the contract.

He has the contact
To make such an impact,
And keep the house intact.

Let him burst the bubble
And burry along the cable,
For us to be comfortable.

Please allow him to subtract
All the junk and abstract.

Remember he was the vice
So he knows the price
Let us toss the dice
And truly get it nice,
Other than the lice.

So if you go for the rice
You may have it twice
And still freeze like ice.

Now hear the bell

Hear well, that duty calls
We must break the walls
And get out of the halls
Whether in spring or falls.

## CLOSE TO HELL

I have been here praying for heaven
Hoping to catch a glimpse of paradise
But men, mortal men surround the gate
They chase me close to hell.

I have been here praying for heaven
Believing to climb up to see God
But men, mortal men mount guard in dishonour
And they stone me close to hell.

Men, underworld humans, mortal men
They swear over their dead bodies
But I know I will make heaven
Yes, I believe, I believe I will see God.

## THESE TINY WINGS OF MINE

With these tiny wings of mine
I would fly above the world,
The sky will feel my feathers.

These tiny toes of mine
They will perch on the clouds,
Heavenly bodies would perceive their scent.

These tiny nails of mine
They will cling, cling and cling
They will grip and hold firm the world.

These tiny colours of mine
They will paint and shine and glitter;
With the rainbow to beautify the sky.

This tiny beak of mine
It will perk and peek at large
It will sing and wake the world
Yes, yes, it will sing loud and steady
It will keep the world awake.

## SERENE

I will be silent and listen
I will listen to myself
I will listen to my heart speak to me.

I will listen to my mind
My loud mind shall call the deep.

I will be quiet to listen to myself
I will listen to my heart
My calm heart will point to love.

I will listen to my head
My still head will hear my mind
I will gather my patches of gold.

Sparkles of diamond, trailing my star
Shinning angels onboard the train
Marching in wonderful apparels,
I will listen to my guardian angel.

Definitely, I will feel the serene
Of course, nothing like siren
Angels, only angels on guard
Peace and tranquil, oh calm still serene!

## LOOK YONDER

Here, I have seen a tortoise
Not in my beautiful torquoise,
Here, I have seen abracadabra
Even as alluring as magenta,
Here, in my favourite coffee
I look yonder like a giraffe.

There, I see gorillas
Moving untoward like guerillas,
Here, the wind is brownish
Whether or not you are stylish,
Yet, I look yonder and yawn
As I wander round the lawn.

This fool you see is a tool
A quiver in the hands of a diver
This witch you see is a pitch
A baller in the palm of the Caller.

A witness amidst unbelievers
A thinker among heathens,
Over land and sea, clime and time
This dove is on motion;
Frictional, centrifugal, gravitational, rotational.

Look yonder, this eagle is from the village square
The gods hear her, the spirits hearken
Harbinger of good tidings

Heralded by seraphs
Upholded by cherubs,
Look yonder, this dwarf is a giant.

## HEAVY DUTY

If a robber can rob a robber plantation then a banner can ban a banana plantation.

If a planter can plant a plantain plantation, then a planner can plan a plant to play.

The champion may not be a heavyweight, but a heavyweight is a champion.

Hence the champagne can campaign for a carpenter, if the drink gets either of you drunk.

The grader can not degrade an earthmover, though it moves like the millipede.

The roller dares not roll away the earth, though it rotates or revolves around the orbit.

The dozer can never doze off, because its sound is parallel to its speed, be it a bull or the bull.

The paver saves the waver, and waiver.

And the excavator that belittles the janitor, cannot on its own honour the tutor.

Let the swamp boogie crown itself the champ, and light up its lamp to stamp the camp, then and only then will the swarm take over.

The engine of an engineer that turned an estate into an artist, has the list as a volunteer and or a deer.

If it takes extreme discoveries to move the earth, then you are a heavy duty. Be your duty heavy or light!

## THE DRAIN

It can curve to the west, to send away waste
It can bend to the east, to blend with the end
That's how life models us even on the drain.

You wear blue and white, to glue to the site
You take a walk at work, to wake your stake
That's how the clue can talk to the lake.

Modelling on the drain, modelling a drain
Training the model, come rain come shine
Still, the porcupine is never her concubine.

This tutelage can rear a partridge
And such privilege can raise a village,
Hence we weave silk with money to make milk and honey.

This drain is not to drain us
We will focus the rain, and water
So that we filter both the former and the latter.

My blue, my honour
My purple, my pride
This land is out to bless, so blessed to bless
To bless this blessing of a blessed a child.

The modelling drain, and the modelling artist
Coping on copes of hope, wearing robe of emancipation.

Physical education on my t-shirt,
Wearing a smile in perpetual honour to Dad.


## BAMBOO

I come from the moon
I am not a baboon.

Do not kill my kangaroo
Lest you meet your waterloo.

I am a bamboo
Straight, strength and stability.

As bright as the noon
I am from the moon,
Don't kill my kangaroo.

Stronger than the Rambo
It's not a taboo,
Do not touch my tampoo.

Inside my cocoon
I have my shampoo,
I will keep the tempo
And you will get my memo.

I am not a baboon

Don't burst my balloon,
I fear the shadow of sorrow
Because this hollow is my pillow.

The moon is loud in the cloud
Hence never in the crowd.

Don't kill my kangaroo
You will meet your waterloo,
I am a buffalo
Sweeping the streets of Limpopo.

Hundred, a hundred percent
Flamingo, bingo and Virgo
Don't kill my kangaroo,
You will meet your waterloo.

Low, low and low below
Go, go, and good to go
This buffalo is from the moon
Do not kill her kangaroo
Lest you meet your waterloo.

Bright, right and mighty night
Sight, tight and light flight,
This bamboo is standing straight
Support, pillar, rollercoaster.

# THE JETTY

We are vessels, vessels of honour
The channels through which to anchor,
As we chisel and hustle and whistle.

Of this shore, we line and aline
Lining offshore, and onshore
To refine, refill, discharge and recharge.

We are vessels, vessels to anchor
On anchors of honour
To honour ashore, as aforementioned.

This Jetty is weighty
It is not for something dirty,
Rather for hefty men with lofty heights
Swimming farther than Brussels, for mussels.

Black and yellow, red and white
To pass yonder for brass,
Not to encompass with gas
Rather to have a glass of water
To wine and dine with the mass.

As pretty as this Jetty
As lengthy as not to be petty
Yet a city on such hill
It's a pity; cannot till.

We have not come to steal

Instead let us heal
For no meal is ever enough
Because the real deal is nature is amazing!

The black gold is never old
Sold or told, it is still bold
Cold or hot, rot it never will
For this fold pays huge bill
Hence the driller, needn't drift
For soft is never the gift.

## THE CONTAINER AND THE CONTENT

I am not my hair
I am not the skin
I am the soul that lives within:
In India Arie's words.

This soul could be in a brown skin
It could be in a yellow coat
As well could be in a purple shirt
Or a navy jeans, the soul lives within.

The container is strong, and solid
But the content is to diffuse,
It will evaporate, into the air
So that the world would perceive, and inhale.

The container is but a vessel
Empty, noisy, rusty and decay-able
But the content is the material.

The container and the content
The container could be cunning
The content might be contagious
Container is body, content is soul.

Containers are collections
Contents are coaches
The content of the container is a conversation
The container of the content is the community.

I am not my hair
I am not the skin
I am the soul that lives within,
I am a brown skin
In a purple shirt
And a blue jeans.

I will walk away from trouble, troubling the container
And I will move farther from shame, shameful content.

## THE EVEREST

Of the hills we climb and the valleys we succumb
Of the wills we succeed and the bills we surmount,
These heights frighten we, the pilots.

Rigging to right the tough edges
And running the race of rough faces
Smooth ridges rift our swift chase.

Spirals of oscillation and scintillating spines
Turbines of dams and banks that bank aquarius
Fins and gills always chill the tail.

These Everests gain wings and wind up our wounds, waylaying innocent dorphins,
Yet tigers trigger up and overhaul kingdoms
How dare heights get frightened!

The mighty stroke that choke the woke, and broke the smoke like joke
Sands of time, tastes of salt, salty waters that blame the rain and windy plains that harm the table.

Rungs of ladders weigh heavily on the soil
Roots of trees destroy and debase the earth,
Roofs of huts hit and hurt, heating up pillows and heads
Pulling pranks that rank the bank and tank like plank.

You climb the Everest, with interest in chest, yet you fail to bail the hail and still hail the rail.

How dare heights frighten!

Rugged rider, revealing reels and wheels. Ruling raw and reddened roads.

Deserts bearing waters of flourishing wine, interwoven in hearts of pure line
But Oasis redeem sanity and sanctuary, in altars of consecrated chalices.

Dare the tare, tar the bar, this everest seems secretive and selective!

I see that tall fountains don't keep up with the mountains, rather they fall short of certain curtains and patterns.

Tell them that's why we patrol aimlessly, flying without wings!

# DARK AND LOVELY

From the savannah, to the sahel, to the mangrove, we are dark and lovely.

Landlocked, river-bound, moonlighted or sun-shone, we are still dark and lovely.

From the wilds of Kenya, to the rivers of Senegal, from the lakes of Ethiopia to the shores of Uganda, across to the borders of Rwanda, I bet we are dark and lovely.

Call us apes, chimpanzees, monkeys, or camels, we are stallions and horses, and thousands of chariots, so dark and lovely.

Diamonds are in these swamps, gold is beneath these rocks, we burn coal and freeze pearls, just so that you realize we are dark and lovely.

We walk along the South, we bear the North, we stretch to the West, and gather up to the East, we are so African, dark and lovely.

In between walls, bamboos, dirt and unfinished businesses, we raise, rise and ride even in the dark, yet so lovely too.

In the coasts of Ghana, and heights of Tanzania, within the capes of Zambia, and valleys of Zimbabwe, along the paths of Liberia, and the routes of Gabon, yes in the deep roots of Cameroon, we are Africa, so endowed, amazingly dark and lovely.

Among the pyramids of Egypt, the plantations of Congo, the woods of Malawi, the nuts of South Africa, the sheds of Lesotho, and the mountains of Nigeria, we are preciously dark and lovely.

We are tongues and tribes, regions and religions, yet we are Africa, so dark and lovely.

We dance with the gods and dine with the celestial.

We are spirits, immortal and yet imperfect, look beyond our skin!

We are dark and lovely because the Almighty and all-knowing God made us so...so dark and lovely.

## HAPPY INTERNATIONAL WOMEN'S DAY

In a world where the weather is neither favourable nor friendly, we hold dear to the blocks, the blocks with which to build our future.

Dark environment, harsh atmosphere, we hold on to the bricks that would be together with the sticks, sticks that stick and help pick the pieces of us.

These blocks frame us, they tame us, they support our game, and wipe the shame when we walk, work and wake from the lame.

They form the rock where the flock dock and wait upon the clock. The clock that breaks the lock, and suck up those who mock.

It will block the blockade, and buckle the blockage, buttressing the bull and bundling the bulky bully.

Work in progress, a pinch of hopeful congress, the hope of tomorrow. Labouring not in vain.

Take this to heart, we mould to be moulded. And we build to be built.

The guilt has built, the innocent has innovated, and the acquitted has acquired, yet it is only the blocks that can chain their blocks.

When we face down and ponder on the happenings, events take us round the bush, dropping us at every corner of the mess, to show us that being a woman is divine... divine in a world devoid of celestial humans.

But then, we must hold on to the blocks as we build, because we are not building for the ordinary!

*Happy International Women's Day to my mum, sisters, nieces and all the good females around the world*

## SITTING ON THEIR MANDATE

This green vegetation has a sandy soil, it is barely fertile and rarely productive.

My jeans has not been able to shield the pain of these rods, my buttocks are hurting.

Their mandate is a hundred percent painful, standing on it is tiring, sitting on it is piercing.

See how the sun is brazenly blinding. And the blueness of wears is not helping. My skin is feeling it, high. The rays of the wavelength is hard to calculate.

I did not mandate any Tin. The land of gold fought for mandela. That's a mandate and man recalls the date.

How long shall I sit on this edge in pain, facing the sun directly in dazzling pretence and piercing pain?

Sharp edges of numberless agony, blunt hooks of disheartening loss, crazy crowd of loud misfortune, lazy tribes of crowded misfit.

How long shall I sit here and watch the strong retain the spoil?

Upon your mandate, you are tired to stand. Stand alone, this fictitious strength has to carry you. Attention! Stand at ease!

These piercing rods and puncturing irons are oxidizing the ions. These cathodes and anodes are winding down windmills, and the sawmills no longer have woods.

A great farmer can mess up a land if he cultivates in the desert. This farmer does not even know the names of crops, and the types of soil. Who made him a farmer? What makes him a farmer?

Duty calls. But there is hunger in the land. This mandate is not a man's date. The truth is it is not timely. The dare, is, it is the masses' silence. I didn't mandate you. Why am I sitting here, suffering?

This long bench of sharp edges, pinching the people and cracking their skin will go blunt on its own. Watch out.

It's a hundred percent blue, blue pain.
Where then is the beauty? If blue has turned to bulaba.

It will favour me and my family. On this mandate we shall stand. On this mandate we still stand. It is my turn, our turn. Grab it, snatch it and run with it.
Usain Bolt didn't even snatch a baton.

I hope your legs are neither hurting nor numb, because some legs are already shaking when the race is round the clock, more than a marathon.

Mandela, this is not how your mandate looked like, because twenty-seven years of isolation and hard labour couldn't have produced anything short of the people's president.

The unfortunate mandatory part is that everyone is either standing or sitting on this mandate. Shaking legs, hurting buttocks, broken backs, hopelessly renewed.

A mannequin manner of mandate so mannerlessly masterminded for manna.

No wonder the blind people were tremendously amazed when they saw miracles, they marvelled and shouted "what manner of man!"

## THE OTHER SIDE OF LIFE

This is a shame to name
And a tame to a dame,
It is a lame game
And a frame against fame.

A team with no steam
A beam without seam,
And a veteran outside vatican.

Please if we were ever in Rome
Whether abroad or at home,
Please pray for us dear Pope
For this is too hard to cope.

A crucial date in a local boat
A racial fate without moral coat;
A very lame game in shame and blame.

A bell ringer to tell hell,
A cell singer to sell the well,
A blunt axe to fell an iroko.
Who does that?

A market day, perhaps a judgement day
They blew the screw on the pew and crew,
A frame to tame same fame.
Who does that?

The real 'goat' could not float
Junior Pope beyond scope and behind hope
Roped and robed at the other side of life.

A wave can sink a cave
And drink the octave you gave,
Therefore we must pave way to save.

An only child in a guild
Mild, to build from the wild
But even Luke failed the physician
And chose to poke the mortician.

Doctor native to bail the captive
And captain naive to sail the fugitive:

"Bros abeg small small
Na only me dem born
I be the only child
I get three children
And na me go raise them"

Now I ask, who does that from the other side of life?

# FAME IN THE WOOD

Talent is latent because patent is not patient to parent the content.

Honey is abusing harmony because money has become a bedbug in matrimony. A very stormy paradise and gummy garden.

The sag is the swag and the brag is the wag. The rag is the bag, and the drag is the gag because the nag is the lag.

A pain to gain the rain and a disdain to maintain. A vain plain to sustain a main stain that will surely drain fame in the wood.

A cone that will stone you and clone your bone, yet the lone drone will capture you alone without the throne, change the tone, be done and gone with one or none.
Fame in the wood.

Turn the cup, burn him up
Run her over, gun him down
Tear her off, wear him out
A stroke of woke in the wood,
And the horrible joke they spoke.

Living in bondage for money
Things fall apart for honey
Illumination for name
African magic, the game
Black health for wealth,
A frame of fame in the wood.

The wood is the forest
The food not the sweetest
The hood is the largest
The mood not the best
And no good comes from the test
Yet they brood never to rest.

The pest, foretold
The nest, withhold
The guest, to fold the bold
A very cold wood,
Still, famous and callous.

A warm wood of worm
In shapeless form and norm;
Uninformed and deformed.

A lukewarm wood of thorn,
Born, worn and torn.

Horn of restless band
Land of tasteless corn
Burning dust to dust
Razing ash to ash
Fading wind to wind
Because of fame in the wood.

## MY DEAR OLIVIA

Nuts, they have gone with guts
Yet everything they want they get
Please wear this gown,
And protect your crown.

Remember the sacrament of baptism
And the sacredness of olive,
The consecration and confirmation.

My dear Olivia, there is no rivalry
Because thorns were worn on calvary
And vinegars drank at vinegary.

Nakedness could mean madness
Sure, it can never be beauty
For beauty is excellent and wise.

The communion of the soul is with the spirit
While the commonness of the body is with the flesh.

My own Olivia, it takes rudeness to go nude
Hence I love how crude you are.

You will not dance at the marketsquare
For only the mad shamelessly do so.
Olivia, you will dance like King David
It will be lucid, rigid, solid and vivid.

Like jets they fly, like birds they hardly perch

But your own Olivia is small like an ant, yet bite.

The world will love seduction
They will make palace for seductresses,
The world will praise the serpent
And baptize themselves with serpentine spirit.

But Olivia, your baptism is not for darkness
That peace you bear, is divine.

Leaves of blessed green and ripened orange
Fall on fertile ground and germinate
Let no pigs trample on you
For seeds and fruits await harvest.

Olivia, Olivia of St Catharine's, the purple gold
You were anointed for exploits, not to be exploited
You were processed not to be possessed,
Let woman fade, let human grade
Yet I say make room at the upperchamber.

Royal feathers, loyal wings, flights of serene vision
Heights of calm mission
Might of celestial mercy
Splendour of compassion and support
Majesty of candour and glory.

God with us, Immanuel
Yours Lord, Is The Greatness.

## DIAMONDS ARE FOREVER

My Lord Bishop, Dear Blessing
I know it can be very stressing
But please keep on pressing
For there is a grace of dressing.

Dear Blessing, My Lord Bishop
The gallop will launch you to the top
And you will neither drop nor flop,
You will pop up a bookshop
And crop out God's workshop.

For The One, A Venerable
One can also be vulnerable
But there is a ventilation
For the one, of veneration.

Dear Bright, The Venerable
You will not only be a doctor
But also a ventilator
You will mentor the captor
And monitor the sculptor
So, the janitor will be a protector.

A delight also bears the light
So bruise the fight, and cruise the flight,
For a pure sight has been offered for the night.

Dear Bridget, The Triplet

It does not matter your budget
For there is a rainbow magnet
To take you to the colourful target,
And it will interweave every net.

Along The Bridge, I Know You Fret
Yet I bet you are nature's pet
Hence let no regret get any room for the set
As you royally jet on in queenly signet.

It Is A Diamond Blessing,
A bright almond across the bridge.

The Bond Of Triplets Is A Pond
It will always fund the fond
And such blessing will venerate the bridge.

Happy Birthday To The Triplets
Merry Diamond Blessings
And may the triune God ever be with you,
Because diamonds are forever.

# THE TESTIMONY OF A GREEN SOUL

I am not a lawyer
But I have a testimony
I am not a player
But I am a child of destiny.

My spleen is green
But I am not a weed
My screen is seen
But my creed is not greed.

We breed the deed
And heed to feed
Because we need to succeed
And proceed to intercede.

This soul is green
Her sole is green,
This heart is pure
Her art is cure.

The land is life
This clime is strife
The prime is knife
This stand is wife.

I have a testimony
The law is an agony
I am a melody,
This soul is harmony.

My love is alive
It gives more than five
My dove can dive
It can in the wild, thrive.

This is my testimony
Tomorrow is looking good
Because the land is green
And my heart is pure.

I am not Veronica
Neither am I Monica
And I am not their replica.

In this green regalia
I am not a militia.

On green feet and green fingers
On lively fleet and tender gingers
We meet and greet holy harbingers.

Life can happen in a sudden
And we can lighten or darken
When we are bred or made
Life can hurt deep like a steep.

I share in your testimony, Veronica
I care for your destiny, Dominica
I dare the rich Francisca
For bare lies the testimony of Mordecai.

## WE MOVE

The stage is set
Let the dance begin.

The guage is met
Let all the distance win.

The cage is a pet
Let the circumstance reduce to pin.

The garage is in resonance,
Let the substance turn into tin.

The rage is wet
Call the nuisance a sin.

The sage is wise
Let the wage rise.

The age can speak
So manage it to the peak.

Take us to the prime
Where there is no crime.

The stage is set
It is kick-off time.

A branch is of the tree
And the tree is of the forest,
The forest is of a land
And the land is of a people,
A people; noble and humble.

So of lands and climes
Of tongues and tribes,
Of interests and quests
Of mountains and valleys
Of fountains and allies; we move!

A-branch, it is your turn,
Yes, it is your turn,
We move!

You will not dance at the marketsquare
For only the mad shamelessly do so.
Olivia, you will dance like King David
It will be lucid, rigid, solid and vivid.

## THE RAJIS

Valuation is the goal
Raji is the goat.

Taxation is the deal
Ade has the seal.

Management is the key
The Rajis got some whiskey.

Development is the game
Ade is not lame.

Survey is the plan
Raji is the man.

Unity is the vision
Ade is on the mission.

Love is the code
The Rajis are the mode.

Awareness is the ladder
Ade is on the radar.

Anambra is the branch
The Rajis are here to launch.

Leadership is about to sail,

And fellowship will prevail.

Associate with the wave
The Rajis are here to save.

Graduate with the tide
Ade, is far and wide.

School in the field
For the Rajis have the shield.

Honour in concord
And a harbour in one accord.

The Rajis fan the flame
The Rajis bear the name
The Rajis keep the fame
So let the Rajis tame the shame.

## THE VERACITY OF A NOUN

Some times, I marvel at the audacity of foolishness and wonder if courage was silly.

Some times, I ponder further and meditate deeper on the law of shallowness and floatation.

There are times I get confused trying to understand the gravitational pull and viscosity even when I am not in the stratosphere.

Yes, some other times, I travel to trace the race to see if the pace was really laced in grace or a panting face seeking for some brace.

There are times I cringe realizing boldness was actually stupidity.

That time, I frown at tenacity and appear to caution the will and freedom of expression.

My ears have heard the timid echo of vibration and questioned if nuance was nuisance.

When I see myself doubting if success was a blessing or a curse, then I draw from a raw saw that the law does not require a noun to name a person, place, animal or thing.

Whenever I see a celebrity as the opposite of dignity, and opportunity to be the reverse of integrity, then I know that a porous circle without circumference is prone to attack and bound to take a formless shape as soon as possible.

Hence, as errors appear on mirrors, so I believe that horrors are parallel to honours.

Nonetheless, in this era of variety, I can dig a trench for aloe vera and bench the people, then drench myself to resort in a portland, seaport, heliport, airport, or plot of accommodation.

On that note, I want to say this, if there is any way I have missed it, if there is any how I am missing it, if there is any where I will miss it, please forgive me, because I am only testing or naming the veracity of a noun.

# EXTRAORDINARY

I am a flute
I can't be mute.

I am cute
And also acute.

I am a parachute
flying to paradise,
I am not a parasite.

I am a paragon,
call me a dragon.

I am a sun
and also a gun,
you can have me run.

This goddess is a rainbow
and too a moonbow,
she mows even bows and arrows.

I sail even on the rail
and hail my tail,
I tell you my mail is my nail.

The blues navigate me
the dews facilitate me
and the clues dictate loud

for the glues to dissolve in the cloud.

This vessel is sacred
to ship ships in shipments
and parcel parcels in parcels.

Nature is awesome and handsome
neither cumbersome nor burdensome
yet men are troublesome, worrisome and lonesome.

So pay the piper for the tune
or have the prune.

My tone is in my bone
and my clone is also a drone
because this flute is extraordinary.

# IGNITED

Look, among men and women
He is more than ten
So book him a pen
And watch him compose the hen.

He is a royal scribe
From a noble tribe
He can grind and wind
And purposefully find the mind.

He is in concord
To keep the record
Just give him a nod
And watch him break the rod.

Calm, gentle, and articulated
Kind, humble and principled,
Ignatius is a star-plus.

## THREE YEARS IN THE BIG HEART

Three years in the big heart
And more years to tread this path,
Bit by bit, we share the part
Turn by turn, we trade the mart,
Hopefully in good life and sound health.

The rough edges, God prunes
And the tough stages, He tunes.

Of rifts, sources lift
And against drifts, resources gift.

The big heart, nature thwarts
And the fig art, structure starts.

Of nights that light our sight,
And of nights that lighten our fight;
Please lead kindly light.

Of nights that fight our right
And of nights that frighten our height,
Please lead kindly light!

Of nights that prey on our prayers
And of nights that feast on our beasts,
Please lead kindly light!

Strength, for the length ahead
And help, to not mistrust the perishable.

Safe, in snares and lures
Sound, in tares and cures
Please protect, provide, and procure
Lest, amidst plenty we lack still.

Today, I turn three here
Under the shadow of the Almighty,
Happy third anniversary to me,
In a strange and wonderful land;
Of milk and honey, nature and culture.

Hence, on this rogation Sunday
I join the hymnist to sing:

Thine is the loom, the forge, the mart,
　The wealth of land and sea;
The worlds of science and of art,
　Revealed and ruled by thee.

# THE LANDMARK OF EVENTS

He is not from Denmark
Rather from the tiny dot
And that is the benchmark
For him to surely rot.

He bears a birthmark
That is too, very dark
Hence he can not bear the ark
Or play around the park.

Hark, let the dog bark
We plot how to kill the shark
And cook it hot in our pot,
Then toast along the coast.

We feed the glutton with cotton
And send the baboon to lagoon,
We are the core shore,
We roast and boast.

No toad will use the road
We drug the frog to hug the bug
And that is true smarkdown.

This hunt is haunt
The taunt continues for revenue
A cross and the crux
The hallmark of pain,
It is that plain, a sure pattern.

If you rise, we ride you
If you fall, we wall you
If you call, we curse you.

The landmark of events
Inert perverts and experts
Concentrated solvents and solutions
Molten lava melting natural resources.

He is not from Denmark
Rather from that tiny dot,
In case he missed the war
We serve him our weapons, raw.

Queen of the coast,
The marine highway
Subways, walkways, airways, waterways
We are the damn ways.

A land that forbids dreams
A clime that rottens visions.

Eclipse of time and tide
Eclipse of wave and current.

Bridges of loss in gross
Ridges of boss and toss
A stingy fate, a clingy destiny.

But the sun surely does rise

The fool knows, also the wise.

A dice infected with lice pays the price
Because a cone always points to the sky.

This event is a landmark
It may appear like a landslide
But it will give a new landscape
For a mighty landing.

In law, there is no in-law
With the law, all is under the law
But when natural and man-made laws collide
Nature always takes its course
And leave man the discourse.

The valuation, demolition, and compensation
All lie on the rainy plain in pain.

## THE EMPIRICAL FORMULA OF TIN

Let me tell you a tale
Don't be scared of my veil,
I have a very long tail
Just anchor on the vale.

My kinsman is a blue whale
We are neither sick nor pale
Weigh him on any scale
We are that quick and thick.

An emperor is a conqueror
And a major does not minor in inferior.

Now, let me tear the mask
We have a broken flask
Which is neither cold nor hot
Yet, our goldmine is in the pot.

See, Ishmael sent in a worrisome mail
And, Luke had gone lukewarm.

The numerical strength will not feed you
And political correctness will not save you,
The street is down on wounded feet
And the farm is dead in harmful charm.

The spherical catastrophe will envelope the rich
While the global hypocrisy will wrap the poor
The organized crime will indict the innocent

While the neutralized clime will taste the reagent.

The tin is to win
But the tax will not wax
This long walk to freedom may end in bondage.

The iron ore has more
And the cornmeal cannot heal
The subsidy looks like comedy
And the loan is gearing towards tragedy
The remedy is a different trajectory.

The central banking is dishing cerebral meningitis
It looks like the double ticket has cut.

A regular is spectacular in a particular collar
And a circular in a secular lane is already profane,
This ticket is full of crickets.

The peninsula needs so much solar not penicillin
Because the polar will heat the molar and premolar
So watch well, see the ticket is kicking some buckets.

The empirical formula is for the newborn
But the freeborn is impressing the empress
While the airborne is flying up and down.

A blue bird with hands in the air singing its anthem
Wait for its wings in the pocket for a rocket science.

The green vegetation may be barren

The black soil could be fertile
But look up for miracle
If you must get to the pinnacle.

This tin appears expired
So whatever must have transpired
Humans never so desired
Hence men so much required,
However, wolves far less delivered.

Again, the green vegetation may be barren
And the black soil could be fertile,
So pray for some miracle
If you wish for the pinnacle.

## PENTECOST

No matter how robust the locust
There will be a thrust on its crust
For we trust an outburst;
Yes, against lust and rust.

When we pen the cost of holocaust
And weigh a frust from pentecost;
Then we realize the dust is a must.

Our hope is alive
For lively is the Comforter
Yes, faithful the Saviour
And fruitful the promise.

No wonder the hymnist was overwhelmed in that realm singing:

Oh spread the tidings 'round
Wherever man is found,
Wherever human hearts and
human woes abound',
Let every Christian tongue
Proclaim the joyful sound:
The Comforter has come!

The Comforter has come
The Comforter has come
The Holy Ghost from heav'n

The Lord's dear promise giv'n;
Oh spread the tidings 'round
Wherever man is found
The Comforter has come!

## STONE OF HELP

It will rain for our gain
And wash plain the stain,
Tongues of fire shall inspire
And never tire to burn the quire.

The fire to spur the shire
And the horse for victory
Yes, for the course of history.

Tongues to reverse all wrongs
And fire to ignite the lighters;
A pentecost to rekindle the soldiers.

The stone that atones
The tongue of fire, a consuming fire
The harmony and the attorney
A pillar of fire and the fourth man in the fire.

The stone of help: our help in ages past.

The throne of grace: our hope for years to come.

The tone of peace: our shelter from the stormy blast.

Yes, the tune of life: and our eternal home.

So like Samuel, we commemorate this stone of help; Jehovah Ebenezer...

Surely, that same God who maketh war to cease.

**TAKE YOUR FLOWERS**

High, high up the towers
Blessings rain from all lovers,
Deep down, down the covers
Christi reigns in you; His powers.

Come, come, take your flowers
For as thorns pierce our horns;
So do roses beautify our noses.

Take your flowers, Mama in bethel
Go, plant them even in brothels
For a mother can never love less.

Fly high and spread your wings
Oh sing, those melodies dear nightingale
And teach the mockingbird.

## PENCIL IN THE HAND OF THE CREATOR

When I was a kid, I always told my family that my name was "Ngozi Nderika".

I also told the headmistress same, the day my mum took me to enroll into the primary school.

Who was Ngozi Nderika, by the way?

She was my favourite NTA presenter, newscaster, broadcaster .....

When I grew up, listening to Cosmo FM made me develop more flare and passion for broadcasting.

In fact, Cosmo FM trained me even without knowing me or having any contact with me.

I always imagined myself doing every thing a presenter could do just by being addicted to Cosmo FM.

In school, I began writing. And in my final year, the school bore her mass communication studio.

I applied and got instantly invited to come take the news/paper review at noon, after I must have finished from the day's lecture... after being screened/auditioned by the rector, his deputies, some HODs and lecturers.

I continued like that until after my defense, and got a vacation job as a presenter there at masscom studio, 105.5 radio polynek, while waiting for my call-up letter for NYSC.

In school then, I was paired sometimes, with the school orator, the then Dr. Anumihe, during occasions and functions.

I remember anchoring the swearing-in ceremony of the SUG executives, (the year behind us)

I remember interviewing one Dr. Ngozi Osuagwu, a US trained lady, representing the former minister of education, Dr. Igwe Ajah Nwachukwu.

I also remember taking a black American's citation, Renee Clark Thompson..... (something like that)

Going by all that, I thought my flight would be hitch-free and my landing, sure, smooth and rosy.

That's by the way, though.

When I returned from the national youth service, I visited Cosmo FM Enugu, to submit my CV.

I also went to some stations in Awka, Owerri, Port Harcourt,... to try my luck.

None worked out.

Well, I am here writing and publishing. Living my partial dream. Though poor and wretched, but then, I am burning my passion.

In terms of relationship too, we thought if you kept yourself, be alone, and wait on God, you would have secured a direct visa to heaven, but we found out people cohabit and build heavens on earth.

We also thought marriage would be according to who we are, the life we live, and the prayers we make, the seeds we sow, the sacrifices we render, and that line, little did we know that life was and is a mystery... far beyond imaginations, thoughts, beliefs, prayers,...

We also thought virgins must be fruitful, but here we are, watching virgins go barren and those without wombs bearing dozens.

Many a time, it's not about dreaming, praying, wishing, waiting or living upright. Rather, about factors and forces that govern the universe, because we are nothing but pencil in the hand of the Creator....

No wonder King Solomon concluded thus;

"I have seen something else under the sun: The race is not to the swift or the battle to the strong, nor does food come to the wise or wealth to the brilliant or favour to the learned, but time and chance happen to them all."

**BLIND BAT**

See how you spread like a parachute
Pretending to be in motion
But you are actually mute
And causing commotion.

See how tiny your legs
Yet you use them as pegs.

Blind bat of fat mind
Black owl that can't crawl
Dark hawk of greedy gain.

Eyeballs of wild sockets
Large pockets of stolen balls,
Up above dropping shits in bits.

Lean, straight and unclean
Lined, underlined with no spine
Like an umbrella for Cinderella
Yet, big eyes that can't see.

Sit or stand, they mandated
Fit the band, they relegated
Hit the heat, beat the bit
The seat, the feat, all in defeat.

Weightless, and in flight mode

Useless, the deceitful code.

A walker named a worker
A stalker named the locker
A hawker called a hatcher
A mocker called a mother.

Wide hands like a friend
Hide and seek, like a kid
Broad shoulders like a man
Spacious arms as for alms
But large net like cobwebs.

Blind bat of spread wings
Tossing high in those swings
Rusting rings and bruising kings
Burning strings and ruining springs.

## ROW THE BOAT

Dust your coat, row the boat
Gently down the stream
A wonderful team
To lead the dream.

Let every goat stay afloat
Humbly through the sea
Fairly in the wee
Be the bee, give honey
Flee not with the fee.

Row the boat, don't drench our coat
We all shall float, and never gloat.

Gently down the stream
Strongly lay the beam,
Through the sea to pick the pea
Mildly with the storm
Firmly on the norm.

Form the form,
Fade the worm
Brighter in the dark
Mightier in the night.

Link the grips, hold our hips,
Guide the chips, guard our ribs

Sew the zips and sail the ship.

Use the tips, make the trips
Drop the drips, lest they strip
Gently row the stream
Stormy waves, troubled tides
Galloping rides, evil caves
Just row, mildly shall we go
Row, row, tenderly the boat,
Gently, mildly, down the stream.

Across the sea, over the shore
We shall plant and fill the store
If we simply row down the world.

## FROM GRASS TO GRACE

Life can shatter like glass
And lay you down on the grass,
Life can blunt your brass
And stunt your dance of jazz
Yes, life can ruin you to carcass
But grace can win you the race.

Life can shunt your bass
And hunt your ass,
Man is bound to fail
He can wail and ail,
For he is frail and fragile
Yet, he can sail to prevail.

Lace him up for some brace
Space him on more pace
There, grace will be in place.

The masses are not asking for much
The people are not tasking at such,
The land has a lot for lunch
Yet, leaders starve all in bunch.

If a man could be so a patriot
Flying high in passion
Moving around with compassion
Outdoing those compatriots

Then, grace can pin his face.

It takes zeal to make a deal
The local league can hit their colleague
So heat up the polity, and beat the tenacity
Let us move from grass to grace,
Because we can. Yes, we can.

## FARE THEE WELL

We are here to buy and sell
When to leave, we can not tell
Hence we must watch how we dwell,
Short or long, rough or well
We dismiss when we hear the bell.

Life beyond, is very rare
So fear not how you would fare
March on, forget pain and care
For as sorrows boldly lay bare
And troubles deeply do stare;
Harvest time shall win the tare.

Fare thee well, golden voice
It could never have been our choice
But we pray in heaven, you rejoice.

Rest easy, away from the swelling hell
Harp among those harpers of gold
We bid thee well, Mama Ijaw
Christ Church will miss you, raw.

## COME RAIN

O come pure rain
Wash my heart off pain
And give me fruitful plain.

O come rich and holy rain
Wet my soul in gain
And bless my land in not vain.

O blessed rain, wake my spirit from disdain
And spot me from each stain.

Shower in full and not in half
Come, O clean rain, pour from above
And sprinkle on this mortal calf.

O rain, love, true, perfect love
Rain upon me, and the world
Spirit of rain, O rain, rain and reign
A thorough cleanse, a total peace.

## DEAR MALAWI

Dear Malawi, reaching for the mast
We woke up to a stormy blast,
A whole crew and cast
In a twinkle, now in the past.

Dear brother of motherly compass
We mourn the weight and mass
Wailing for this voyage
Lining in pain of passage.

Better teams of wounded toes
In bitter tears and dead woes,
Loops of misery and agony
Troops conquered in harmony.

Fate, misty and cloudy
Date, nasty and rowdy
State; dizzy and moody.

Dear Malawi, poor bright son
Finger on the trigger, and ginger the tiger
Hands on gun, eyes on the sun
Arise and shine, for victory shall be won.

## DEAR ABRAHAM LINCOLN

Dear Abraham Lincoln, the government of the people is planting hunger for the people to harvest famine.

Dear Abraham, the government of the people is killing the people by the people. They are choking the people.

Dear Lincoln, that government of the people is solely out against the people, they are suffocating the people.

Dear Abraham Lincoln, faith is bribing fate and the demon is corrupting races. That demon is crazy!

When a caged white dove or pigeon refuses to fly upon its release, what else could be more signalling?

A few crew grew in the stew and the new pew drew the dew and flew to sew. The demon is crazily caressing the people!

Dear Abraham Lincoln, you wrote to your son's teacher, right?

You asked his teacher to teach him that it is more honourable to fail than to cheat. Abraham dear, I am your son, from what I have seen, let me tell you that that professor compromised.

You asked him to teach him that ten cents earned is more valued than a dollar found. Again, I am your son, I want to tell you that that teacher inflated the dollar.

You asked the teacher to teach your son to have faith in himself. That teacher is professing virus, bribery and corruption. There is no faith, no patience, and no honour left.

Dear Abraham Lincoln, the professor didn't tell you how he manufactures numbers and figures in the name of democracy and democratic elections?

Well, when Lucifer fell, man fell. The walls of Jericho fell, the tower of babel fell, and kingdoms fell too.

Perhaps, that was why Isaac Newton discovered why an apple fell too, and he called it the force of gravity.

Hitherto, we have prayed for manna to fall because the government of the people, by the people and for the people, seems to be anti-people.

Dear Abraham Lincoln, do those who serve the people sever and slit their throats or deprive them of their coats in sinking boats?

If you sat like this, looking tired and speechless, then I am lying down, so helpless and hopeless.

**THE PLATINUM QUEEN**

Much elegance in her substance
And a whole grace at her pace.

Vast quality in rarity
Full resistance and resonance.

Cohesion against corrosion
Comprehension against tension,
Fruition upon friction
That is a platinum queen.

A queen that herself did tame
Even along the hall of fame.

A name you can not frame
Praying as she is slaying,
A game for not the lame.

Born with horns of excellence
For morn and eve of existence,
A platinum metal
Lofty and precious citadel.

Seventy is no joke
But by ninety you will poke
And choke the world.

Happy Platinum Birthday to you

I hope you celebrate a centenary.



**THE RAINFOREST**

Tall as the emergent
Call, comes the sun to prevent
But there lies, the canopy
Begging the understory to be windy.

Shrubs, so thick and green
Vegetation; old, young and teen
Like the Amazon needing the ozone
And the congo reaching for the equator.

Rainforests and the mangroves
Salivating for the groove
Habitats in natural state
Revolving around mate and fate.

## DEAR INSPECTOR AND FESTIVAL PEOPLE

I don't like your cigarette
And I don't like your tattoo,
If you rode on a horse
That, is a transportation course.

If your steeze is to sneeze
For the breeze to freeze me
Then I will squeeze and quiz you.

You are a survivor
I am glad you are,
And a projector
I hope you take care.

Whether a festival of the cutest
Or a survival of the fittest
All the razzmatazz and paparazzi
None can colour my mind.

I have clothes that still fit
And lots that no longer do,
But this jacket is twelve years
Dear inspector, I understand your fears.

So calm down, watch me model
This bowel is not a trowel
Hence for your sweat, I have a towel

Each in consonant or in vowel.

Shadows and trees, shades and sheds
Hairy flights and airy sights
Those, all behold an unconventional goddess
 Feeling priceless in her distinct coffee.

## GREENER PASTURES

Lead kindly light, amid the encircling gloom
Even in dry lands, may we bloom
And never see doom,
Water the vegetation
And feed us with greener pastures.

East or west, make green our hand
North or south, bake the teeming land
Up or down, take off bleeding stand
In or out, shake off greedy band,
Lead us to the greener pastures.

Nature dear, hear us tear and wear
In red or black, stir and cheer us
In plain or plane, in fear or gear
In rear or rare, please care and dare.

In valleys and in mangroves
In rainforests and in deserts
In Sahels and in Savannahs
In dams, in oasis, in seas and oceans
In fountains, in and mountains
Quicken our mortals in sceptres
And make flourish the gardens.

For as winter and autumn must come
And as spring and summer must visit

Hence flowers must blossom.


**UNDER THE MOONLIGHT**

Come, let's play together
It's night already, and the air is warm
The breeze is cool, friendly and fine
And the moonlight is firm, and strong.

Let's play together under the moonlight
Let me tell you tales and fantasies
Fantastic flavours of alluring glamour
In honour and lowly humour.

Birds are singing, and chattering
Hear me too, sing along with them
I hate cage, and I don't like rage
That's why I am a sage with my wage.

Love me, let me live in you
Live through me, let me love you right
Let quiet gardens whisper our names
As moons brighten and light up our ways.

I see footsteps in paths unknown
I hear footmarks in lands beyond
I feel footprints in worlds to come
Hello darling, our feet shall tread ahead.

**KEEP GOING**

Hello dear, keep going
Under the sun and in the rain
In the shade, and on the sun
Hard way or clear path
Walk, work and keep wake.

In wings high or tires hard
Flying speedily or racing slow
Walk, work, keep going.

Lands, strong and painted scopes
Landscapes, hard or hardened lines
Floors, flowered or slippery lanes
Work, Walk, keep trucking.

Lone, lonely, alone or aligning
Lean, lanky and lacking strength
Walk well and work fine.

The blues shall melt the sky
The browns shall move the land
The greens shall heal the earth
The whites shall appease the heaven
The reds, shall enliven the dead
The yellows shall please the universe
And the blacks shall raise creation.

Walk, focus, and march on
Work, locus is the starch done.

Before you, is the workload
Behind you, is the beauty
Beyond you, is the walk of fame
Beside you, is the bag of fortune.

Distractions can be deceitful
Dislocations can be painful
Delusions can be lustful
Dispositions can be vengeful,
Walk, then work, I say.

## I AM NOT A ZOMBIE

I am not a zombie
I have an independent mind
I question every thing.

I am not a zombie
I doubt every move
I think wider not straight.

I am not a zombie
I ponder deeper
I envisage impossibilities.

I am not a zombie
I am flesh and blood
I imagine beyond boundaries.

I am not a zombie
I travel in my spirit
I search for answers.

I am not a zombie
I wonder upon wonders
Because I am a living soul.

I am not a zombie
I imagine crazy things
Because it is a wonderful world.

I am not a zombie
No need to believe in my quest
I wander off the cliff.

I am not a zombie
My mind is expansive
I stretch above the permissible.

I am not a zombie
I am elastic
I dare elasticity and inelasticity.

I am not a zombie
I am curious
I inquire abnormally.

I am not a zombie
I am very weird
In worlds cruelly wild.

I am not a zombie
Don't force me to swallow
My throat is choosy.

I am not a zombie
I am not envious
I am not a zombie
But I could be jealous.

I am not a zombie

I am selective
I am not a zombie
I am cautious.

I am not a zombie
I am conscious,
This may sound ridiculous
But I am not a zombie.

I am not a zombie
I am calculative
I am not a zombie
I am intuitive.

Go with the bandwagon
I am not a zombie
Go with the whirlwind
I am not a dust.

I am not a zombie
My soul is alive
I am not a zombie
I cherish sanctity and sanity.

I am not a zombie
I flow with the rare
I am not a dummy
I bleed blood.

I am not a zombie
I have values
I am not a zombie
I have principles.

I can't be a zombie
I have culture
I am not a zombie
I dream future.

I am not a zombie
I have senses
I am not a zombie
I am extraordinary.

I am not a zombie
I am unique
I am not a zombie
I am spectacular.

I have eyes, let me see
I have ears, I hear
I have nose, I perceive
I have skin and hand
I touch and feel,
I have mouth and tongue,
I taste and speak.

I am not a zombie

I don't tie or barricade my head
I am not a zombie
I can't pause my thinking faculty.

I wander, I wonder
I imagine, I think
I create, I assemble
I import, I build
I am not a zombie
Allow me explore my tiny head.

Discover lines across the mirrors
See tricks and beauties
Risk normalcy and conventions,
Because conveniences can be limiting.

I am not a zombie
Don't be surprised,
My doubts are boundless
I barely get attached.

I am not a zombie
It's okay if you hate it
I am not a zombie
Life is not a pushover.

It is not a walkover
So I won't be a leftover.

I don't want to be a zombie
Though I know nothing,
But you can call me a fool
Because I am old-school.

## Mmap New African Poets Series

If you have enjoyed *Taurai Amai,* consider these other fine books in the **Mmap New African Poets** Series from *Mwanaka Media and Publishing:*

*I Threw a Star in a Wine Glass* by Fethi Sassi
*Best New African Poets 2017 Anthology* by Tendai R Mwanaka and Daniel Da Purificacao
*Logbook Written by a Drifter* by Tendai Rinos Mwanaka
*Mad Bob Republic: Bloodlines, Bile and a Crying Child* by Tendai Rinos Mwanaka
*Zimbolicious Poetry Vol 1* by Tendai R Mwanaka and Edward Dzonze
*Zimbolicious Poetry Vol 2* by Tendai R Mwanaka and Edward Dzonze
*Zimbolicious: An Anthology of Zimbabwean Literature and Arts, Vol 3* by Tendai Mwanaka
*Under The Steel Yoke* by Jabulani Mzinyathi
*Fly in a Beehive* by Thato Tshukudu
*Bounding for Light* by Richard Mbuthia
*Sentiments* by Jackson Matimba
*Best New African Poets 2018 Anthology* by Tendai R Mwanaka and Nsah Mala
*Words That Matter* by Gerry Sikazwe
*The Ungendered* by Delia Watterson
*Ghetto Symphony* by Mandla Mavolwane
*Sky for a Foreign Bird* by Fethi Sassi
*A Portrait of Defiance* by Tendai Rinos Mwanaka
*Zimbolicious: An Anthology of Zimbabwean Literature and Arts, Vol 4* by Tendai Mwanaka and Jabulani Mzinyathi

*When Escape Becomes the only Lover* by Tendai R Mwanaka
وَيَسـهَرُ اللَّيلُ عَلَى شَفَتي...وَالغَمَام by Fethi Sassi
*A Letter to the President* by Mbizo Chirasha
*This is not a poem* by Richard Inya
*Pressed flowers* by John Eppel
*Righteous Indignation* by Jabulani Mzinyathi:
*Blooming Cactus* by Mikateko Mbambo
*Rhythm of Life* by Olivia Ngozi Osouha
*Travellers Gather Dust and Lust* by Gabriel Awuah Mainoo
*Chitungwiza Mushamukuru: An Anthology from Zimbabwe's Biggest Ghetto Town* by Tendai Rinos Mwanaka
*Zimbolicious: An Anthology of Zimbabwean Literature and Arts, Vol 5* by Tendai Mwanaka
*Because Sadness is Beautiful?* by Tanaka Chidora
*Of Fresh Bloom and Smoke* by Abigail George
*Shades of Black* by Edward Dzonze
*Best New African Poets 2020 Anthology* by Tendai Rinos Mwanaka, Lorna Telma Zita and Balddine Moussa
*This Body is an Empty Vessel* by Beaton Galafa
*Between Places* by Tendai Rinos Mwanaka
*Best New African Poets 2021 Anthology* by Tendai Rinos Mwanaka, Lorna Telma Zita and Balddine Moussa
*Zimbolicious: An Anthology of Zimbabwean Literature and Arts, Vol 6* by Tendai Mwanaka and Chenjerai Mhondera
*A Matter of Inclusion* by Chad Norman
*Keeping the Sun Secret* by Mariel Awendit
*سِجلٌّ مَكتُوبٌ لتَائه* by Tendai Rinos Mwanaka
*Ghetto Blues* by Tendai Rinos Mwanaka
*Zimbolicious: An Anthology of Zimbabwean Literature and Arts, Vol 7* by Tendai Rinos Mwanaka and Tanaka Chidora

*Best New African Poets 2022 Anthology* by Tendai Rinos Mwanaka and Helder Simbad
*Dark Lines of History* by Sithembele Isaac Xhegwana
*a sky is falling* by Nica Cornell
*Death of a Statue* by Samuel Chuma
*Along the way* by Jabulani Mzinyathi
*Strides of Hope* by Tawanda Chigavazira
*Young Galaxies* by Abigail George
*Coming of Age* by Gift Sakirai
*Mother's Kitchen and Other Places by Antreka. M. Tladi*
*Best New African Poets 2023 Anthology by Tendai Rinos Mwanaka, Helder Simbad and Gerald Mpesse*
*Zimbolicious Anthology Vol 8* by Tendai Rinos Mwanaka and Mathew T Chikono
*Broken Maps* by Riak Marial Riak
*Formless by* Raïs Neza Boneza
*Of poets, gods, ghosts. Irritants and storytellers* by Tendai Rinos Mwanaka
*Ethiopian Aliens* by Clersidia Nzorozwa
*In The Inferno* by Jabulani Mzinyathi
*Who Told You To Be God* by Mariel Awendit
*Nobody Loves Me* by Abigail
*The Stories of Stories* by Nkwazi Mhango
*Nhorido* by Siphosami Ndlovu and Tinashe Chikumbo
*Best New African Poets 10*$^{th}$ *Anniversary: Selected English African Poets* by Tendai Rinos Mwanaka
*Best New African Poets 10*$^{th}$ *Anniversary: Interviews and Reviews of African Poets* by Tendai Rinos Mwanaka
*Best New African Poets 10*$^{th}$ *Anniversary: African Languages and Collaborations* by     Tendai Rinos Mwanaka

*ANTOLOGIA DOS MELHORES "NOVOS" POETAS AFRICANOS 10º Aniversário: Poetas Africanos Da Língua Portuguesa Selecionados* by Lorna Telma Zita and Tendai Rinos Mwanaka
*ABRACADABRA*, by Olivia Ngozi Osuoha
*DES MEILLEURS "NOUVEAUX" POÈTES AFRICAINS 10ᵉ Anniversaire : Poètes africains d'expression française* by Geraldin Mpesse and Tendai Rinos Mwanaka

www.ingramcontent.com/pod-product-compliance
Lightning Source LLC
Chambersburg PA
CBHW070938180426
43192CB00039B/2333